Let's Talk about

The
Holy Spirit

God on Earth in His people today

By Ray Thomas

Introduction

Jesus Christ, the Son of God, came to Earth and lived amongst us. From the age of thirty years old, for the next three years, He ministered, preaching the good news for us, healing the sick, and raising the dead to life.
Then Jesus paid the ultimate price for us, He gave His life to take away the sins of the world.

Three days later Jesus rose again and in doing so defeated death.

For forty days Jesus stayed on Earth with His disciples before He went back to Heaven His mission complete.

Jesus had already said in John 16:7, *"But very truly I tell you, it is good for you that I am going away. Unless I go away the Advocate (the Holy Spirit) will not come to you; but if I go, I will send Him to you."*

Then in acts 1 :4-5 Jesus said, *"Do not leave Jerusalem, but wait for the gift my Father has promised, which you have heard me speak about. For John baptised you with water, but in a few days, you will be baptised with the Holy Spirit."*

So who is the Holy Spirit that Jesus sent to us? That is what we are going to talk about in this book.

Contents

Let's talk about

The Holy Spirit

Before we really get started, let us look at the Holy trinity so we know who is who. It important to get this right so we can understand about the Holy Spirit.

The trinity consists of God the Father, Jesus, and the Holy Spirit, but,

God the Father isn't Jesus, or the Holy Spirit

Jesus isn't the Holy Spirit, or God the Father And the Holy Spirit is not Jesus or God the Father
<u>. But all three together are God</u>.

Totally together, totally in agreement and each with their own Ministry.

That may sound hard to understand but, the example I can use is H2O. Ice is solid, water is
Liquid, and steam is a vapour, but they are all H2O.

In the same way Father, Son, and Holy Spirit are God. I know it is a poor example, but it Helps to make my point.

God the Father makes the decisions and Jesus and the Holy Spirit move in obedience to the Father's will. That of course is a generalisation and there are times when all three work together.
Jesus, in total obedience to the Father, came down to Earth to die on the cross for our sins. In rising from the dead, He defeated death and gave salvation and eternal life to those who accept Him as their Saviour. Now He sits at the right hand of the Father praying for us.

So, who is the Holy Spirit?

From that reading alone we can see that the Holy Spirit is a person not just a force. Some people mistakenly believe that the Holy Spirit is just God's power on the Earth. This is wrong. As I have already said, The Holy Spirit is the third person in the Holy Trinity of the Father, Son and Holy Spirit.

In John 16:13, Jesus said:
"When He, the Spirit of truth, comes, **He** will guide you into all the truth".
Yes, Jesus called the Holy Spirit **He** not it.
Because He is not confined to being in one place only. He is everywhere at once; He is in fact **God on Earth today.**

Because He can be everywhere at once, He can, and does, speak God's will to God's people
Acts 13:1-2 says: "In the church at Antioch there were prophets and teachers: Barnabas, Simeon called Niger, Lucius of Cyrene, Manaen (who had been brought up with Herod the tetrarch) and Saul. 2 While they were worshiping the Lord and fasting, **the Holy Spirit said**, "Set apart for me Barnabas and Saul for the work to which I have called them."

God wanted Barnabas and Saul, (who later became know as Paul) to work for Him, so He sent the Holy Spirit to tell them. God still works in the same way today, calling people to serve Him.
Some people say that they heard an audible voice speaking to them, but usually we don't hear an audible voice; the Holy Spirit talks to our spirit, and somehow, we know that is God speaking to us.
This is what happens when we first give our hearts Jesus. We hear God's word being preached and the Holy

Spirit reveals the truth of those words and convicts us of our sin that we might turn to Jesus for forgiveness.

The Holy Spirit reveals to us who Jesus is and points us to Him. We can see this in Matthew 16, when Jesus asked the disciples who they thought He was, Simon Peter said, "You are the Christ the son of the living God." And Jesus replied, "blessed are you Simon Peter, for this was not revealed to you by flesh and blood, but by my father in Heaven." In other words, by the Holy Spirit.

The Holy Spirit is the most wonderful, most powerful, most loving, most knowledgeable person on Earth, and so much more, yet He is totally obedient to God the Father. He is God on earth today. Because He is Spirit dwelling in Christians to aid us in our Christian walk.

Because He is God, He is almighty. When He comes into our lives He comes with gifts and with fruit, and He leads us into exciting adventures that we would never have dreamt of before. He gives us power and He gives us guidance. So, let's talk some more about this wonderful person.

So, let's take a closer look at
the relationship between God the Father and the Holy Spirit?

The Holy Spirit is the one through whom God does all that is in His heart to do:
In creating and sustaining the world
Genesis 1:2-3 says:
"Now the earth was formless and empty, darkness was over the surface of the deep, and the **Spirit of God was hovering over the waters. And God said, "Let there be light," and there was light."**

And Psalm 104:30 says

"When you send **your Spirit**, they (all creatures) are created."

This is where some people make the mistake that the Holy Spirit is just a power or force used by God. But that is not so. The person the Holy Spirit acted in obedience to God the Father.

It becomes plainer to see that He is a person when we read the next Scripture.

2 Peter 1 verse 21 says: "For prophecy never had its origin in the human will, but prophets, though human, spoke from God as they were carried along **by the Holy Spirit."**

In other words

The Holy Spirit Guided the writers of Scripture.

A mere force could not do that, it takes someone with knowledge.

Things get really exciting when we realise that **The Holy Spirit Provided the Saviour**

Matthew 1:20:21 says:

"But after he had considered this, an angel of the Lord appeared to him in a dream and said, "Joseph son of David, do not be afraid to take Mary home as your wife, because **what is conceived in her is from the Holy Spirit.** She will give birth to a son, and you are to give him the name Jesus, because he will save his people from their sins."

That's right, by miracle power, The Holy Spirit made Mary pregnant with our Lord and Saviour Jesus.

The Holy Spirit is instrumental In Bringing new birth

John 3: 5-8 says:

"Jesus answered, "Very truly I tell you, no one can enter the kingdom of God unless they are born of water and the Spirit. Flesh gives birth to flesh, but **the Spirit gives birth to spirit**. You should not be surprised at my saying, 'You must be born again.' The wind blows wherever it pleases. You hear its sound, but you cannot tell where it comes from or where it is going. **So it is with everyone born of the Spirit."**

What does that mean?

Well, being born of water is our natural birth, as it says ,"flesh gives birth to flesh."

But what about "spirit gives birth to spirit"?
Ephesians 2:1 tells us that before we became Christians "we were dead in our trespasses and sin."
We obviously were not physically dead, or we wouldn't be here.
It means we were spiritual dead and that is why we must be "born again" of the Spirit. Only the Holy Spirit can give us this new spiritual birth.

John 16: 8 says"
"But when the kindness and love of God our Saviour appeared, he saved us, not because of righteous things we had done, but because of his mercy. **He saved us through the washing of rebirth and renewal by the Holy Spirit, whom he poured out on us generously through Jesus Christ our Saviour."**
Isn't it wonderful that God loves us so much that the whole Trinity work together for our Salvation? Hallelujah!

What is the relationship between the Holy Spirit and God's people?

The Holy Spirit has been on the Earth since the Earth was created. In the second verse in Bible, (Genesis 1:2) It tells us that "the Spirit of God was hovering over the waters."

Through out the old testament we see how the Holy Spirit **came upon God's servants anointing them for certain tasks.**

Numbers 16-17 says:

The Lord said to Moses: "Bring me seventy of Israel's elders who are known to you as leaders and officials among the people. Have them come to the tent of meeting, that they may stand there with you. 17 I will come down and speak with you here, and **I will take some of the power of the Spirit that is on you and put it on them.** They will share the burden of the people with you so that you will not have to carry it alone."

Judges 3:9-10 says:

"But when they cried out to the Lord, he raised up for them a deliverer, Othniel son of Kenaz, Caleb's younger brother, who saved them. **The Spirit of the Lord came on him**, so that he became Israel's judge."

1 Samuel 16:13

"So Samuel took the horn of oil and anointed him in the presence of his brothers, and from that day on **the Spirit of the Lord came powerfully upon David."**

As you can see from these few short scriptures, the Holy Spirit on came upon certain individuals who were called to serve God in a special way. He was not poured out on everyone. Nowadays **all** Christians can receive the Holy Spirit.

The prophets who prophesied the coming of Jesus also prophesied that He would be empowered with the Holy Spirit.

That is interesting, isn't it? Nobody prophesied that Jesus would come in His own strength, He laid all that down when He came to Earth as a man. Jesus, when He was on the Earth needed the Holy Spirit.

Isaiah 11:2 says:
"The Spirit of the Lord will rest on him—
 the Spirit of wisdom and of understanding,
 the Spirit of counsel and of might,
 the Spirit of the knowledge and fear of the Lord"

and Isaiah 42:1 says:
(God the Father said) "Here is my servant, whom I uphold, my chosen one in whom I delight; I will put my Spirit on him, and he will bring justice to the nations."

And as always with Biblical prophecy, this prophecy came to pass. Isaiah lived over 700 years before Christ. He had no idea who was talking about or when it would happen, but in faith he prophesied what God gave him to say.
Like Isaiah, we don't need to understand what God is telling us to do, we should just do it.

This Prophecy was fulfilled in Christ

We can read about it in Luke 3:21-22, where it says:
"And as he was praying, (Jesus) Heaven was opened, and the **Holy Spirit descended on him in**

bodily form like a dove. And a voice came from heaven: "You are my Son, whom I love; with you I am well pleased."

It is interesting to see that although Jesus is the son of God, He had no power of His own and had to be filled with the Holy Spirit to perform the miracles that He did. That is explained in Philippians Chapter 2:6-8.
"Jesus Christ, being in the very nature God, did not consider equality with God something to be used or His own advantage; rather, He made Himself nothing by taking on the nature of a servant, being made in human likeness. and being found in appearance as a man, He humbled Himself by becoming obedient to death- even death on the cross."

Yes, when Jesus walked the Earth, it was as a man, just like you and I and He was totally dependent on the Holy Spirit. Isn't that a great example for us?

Jesus clearly understood this about Himself because Luke 4: 14-21teaches us:
Jesus returned to Galilee **in the power of the Spirit**, and news about him spread through the whole countryside. He was teaching in their synagogues, and everyone praised him. He went to Nazareth, where he had been brought up, and on the Sabbath day he went into the synagogue, as was his custom. He stood up to read, and the scroll of the prophet Isaiah was handed to him. Unrolling it, he found the place where it is written: "The Spirit of the Lord is on me, because he has anointed me to proclaim good news to the poor. He has sent me to proclaim freedom for the prisoners. and recovery of sight for the blind, to set the oppressed free, to proclaim the year of the Lord's favour."

Then he rolled up the scroll, gave it back to the attendant and sat down. The eyes of everyone in the synagogue were fastened on him. He began by saying to them, "Today this scripture is fulfilled in your hearing."

Did you see that? He didn't claim to be doing it in His own power, but under the direction of the Holy Spirit.
S, let's get this straight; Jesus, who raised people from the dead, gave sight to the blind, healed the paralysed man, healed lepers and turned no one away who was brought to Him, didn't do it in His own strength, because He had laid that down when He came to Earth. He did it by the power of the Holy Spirit.
He was a man who was totally obedient to His Father in Heaven. It was when He was baptised that the Holy Spirit descended on in the form of a dove, and that was when His ministry began.

If Jesus needed the Holy Spirit to perform His ministry how much do we need Him?
Well the good news is that He is here now, waiting to aid us in the same way He aided Jesus. Isn't that wonderful.

Another point we need to remember is this:
It was the Holy Spirit who raised Christ from the dead.

Isn't that remarkable? Jesus the son of man and son of God was dead in the tomb, he couldn't raise Himself from the grave, if he could, he wouldn't have been fully dead. He needed the powerful Holy Spirit to do it for Him. There are no other forces on Earth able to it.

And here is some more good news for us;

In Romans 8, when Paul is talking to the Christians in Rome, he says, "the same power that raised Christ from the dead is at work in you."

Wow that means us! So much love, so much grace, so much power at work in each of us. How amazing is that? It is awesome! The Holy Spirit is at work within me, within you, within all Christians. There is nothing and no one we need to fear!

That fact that we have the Holy Spirit with us today is a fulfilment of a promise made Jesus before He returned to Heaven.

The Lord Jesus Christ Promised to send us the Holy Spirit

In John 16 Verse 5- 15Jesus tells His disciples,
"But now I am going to him who sent me. None of you asks me, 'Where are you going?' Rather, you are filled with grief because I have said these things. But very truly I tell you, it is for your good that I am going away. **Unless I go away, the Advocate (the Holy Spirit) will not come to you;** but if I go, I will send him to you. When he comes, he will prove the world to be in the wrong about sin and righteousness and judgment: about sin, because people do not believe in me; about righteousness, because I am going to the Father, where you can see me no longer; and about judgment, because the prince of this world now stands condemned.
"I have much more to say to you, more than you can now bear. **But when he, the Spirit of truth, comes, he will guide you into all the truth**. He will not speak on his own; he will speak only what he hears, and he will tell you what is yet to come. He will glorify me because it is from me that he will receive what he will make

known to you. All that belongs to the Father is mine. **That is why I said the Spirit will receive from me what he will make known to you.**"

Now here is an amazing thing. In the old Testament the Holy Spirit only spoke or ministered through certain individuals. That was completely changed after Jesus went back to Heaven. Now the Holy Spirit wants to fill and direct all Christians. That is you and me, and everyone else who is a Christian.

In Joel 2:28-29, He prophecies this wonderful Thing. Talking about the future he gave this prophecy from God,
    "I will pour out my Spirit on all people. Your sons and daughters will prophesy, your old men will dream dreams, your young men will see visions. Even on my servants, both men and women, I will pour out my Spirit in those days."

So let us be clear
When did the Holy Spirit come to live in all God's people?

The Holy Spirit came at Pentecost to the disciples in the upper room.
 In Luke 24:49 Jesus said to the disciples: "I am going to send you what my Father has promised; but stay in the city until you have been clothed with power from on high".

So the disciples obeyed Jesus and stayed together in an upstairs room somewhere in Jerusalem. I wonder how they felt. Did they wonder what the future held for them now that Jesus was no longer with the? Did they feel like giving up hope? Nevertheless, they obeyed Jesus, and forten days they prayed together. None of them could possibly imagine what was going to happen.

We read about it in Acts 2:1-4
"When the day of Pentecost came, they were all together in one place. Suddenly a sound like the blowing of a violent wind came from heaven and filled the whole house where they were sitting. They saw what seemed to be tongues of fire that separated and came to rest on each of them. All of them were filled with **the Holy Spirit** and began to speak in other tongues as the Spirit enabled them."

Wow, can you imagine how they must have felt? One minute they were praying, the next they heard a wind in the room, they saw a fire appear and the fire came to rest on them. What was happening? Suddenly they were talking in foreign languages, and they must of felt such a surge of power within them that they had never known before.

So, who receives the Holy Spirit?

This is the thrilling bit for us, this experience wasn't just for the disciples. God gives Holy Spirit to all who turn from their sin and put their faith in Jesus Christ.
Acts 39, Talking to Christians, says, "The promise is for you and your children and for all who are far off —for all whom the Lord our God will call."

We are the ones who were afar off. He is talking about us and all Christians through every generation, in every tribe and every tongue. The Holy Spirit is God's gift to all of us.

Originally the Jews thought that because they were God's chosen people that the Holy Spirit was for them alone as they were shocked to find out that this wasn't so.

Acts 10-45-46 tells us, "The circumcised believers (the Jews) who had come with Peter were astonished that the gift of the Holy Spirit had been poured out even on Gentiles For they heard them speaking in tongues and praising God."

But by the time Paul was preaching it was an accepted fact that the Holy Spirit was for **all** believers whether Jew or gentile.

WE see this in Ephesians 1:13-14

"And you also were included in Christ when you heard the message of truth, the gospel of your salvation. When you believed, you were marked in him with a seal, **the promised Holy Spirit,** who is a deposit guaranteeing our inheritance until the redemption of those who are God's possession—to the praise of his glory."

To their peril some people thought that the Holy Spirit was just a power that the disciples had somehow attained, that could be bought and sold. This of course isn't true,

The Holy Spirit cannot be bought

Acts 8:18-22 says:
When Simon saw that the Spirit was given at the laying on of the apostles' hands, he offered them money and said, "Give me also this ability so that everyone on whom I lay my hands may receive the Holy Spirit." Peter answered: "May your money perish with you, because you thought you could buy the gift of God with money! You have no part or share in this ministry, because your heart is not right before God. Repent of this wickedness and pray to the Lord in the hope that he may forgive you for having such a thought in your heart."

Neither can He be earned

In His letter. to The Galatians, Paul wrote in Chapter 3 Verse 5
"I would like to learn just one thing from you: Did you receive the Spirit by the works of the law, or by believing what you heard? ...does God give you his Spirit and work miracles among you by the works of the law, or by your believing what you heard?"

Then Paul answered his own question, "He redeemed us ...so that by **faith** we might receive the promise of the Spirit".
So there we have it, the Holy Spirit cannot be bought and cannot be earned. The only way we receive the Holy Spirit, is by faith.

The second dispensation

Accepting Jesus as our Lord and Saviour is the most wonderful thing that could ever happened to us. Our sins are forgiven, we have a friend in Jesus, and we can look forward to spending eternity in Heaven with Him.

Nothing could be better than what Jesus has done for us, and nothing could be more wonderful than His promise of Heaven.

But the Lord knows that we need help to make it through this life and to be able to face each day with courage and strength. That is why He sends us the Holy Spirit.

Some people believe that we receive the Holy Spirit at the moment that we get saved, and up to a point they are right. It was the Holy Spirit who led us to Christ.

But is there a second dispensation of the Holy Spirit? One where we move on from just being saved, but to be vessels of the Holy Spirit, a people of power to be used by God to establish His kingdom on the Earth. Yes! It is called the baptism of the Holy Spirit.

How can we be filled with the Holy Spirit?

Well, first things first, we must be born again Christians. The Holy Spirit is only for Christians, He only comes to those who are following Jesus.

Secondly, we must recognise that the Holy Spirit is an unearned, undeserved gift from God.

That is good news, isn't it? Otherwise, none of us could receive the Holy Spirit.

The next one might seem obvious, but it needs saying; we have to **ask** God to fill us with His Holy Spirit, and we should do it in faith, expecting God to do it.

It says in Luke 11: 13, "If you then, being evil, know how to give good gifts to your children, how much more shall your Heavenly Father give the Holy Spirit to them that ask Him."

How exciting is that? God **wants** to bless us with the Holy Spirit.

Sometimes the Lord does this directly, perhaps when you are in your room praying.
Sometimes God pours out His Spirit on a whole group of people gathered together in prayer, just as He did on the day of Pentecost. There is no middleman involved.

At other times people receive the Holy Spirit by the laying on of hands and prayers of other Spirit filled Christians. In Acts chapter 8 it tells the story of Peter and John visiting the Church at Samaria. Verse 17 says "then Peter and John placed their hands on them, and they received the Holy Spirit".

Dear brothers and sisters who haven't yet received the baptism of the Holy Spirit. I beseech you to earnestly pray for this wonderful gift from God; or if you feel more comfortable, ask someone in authority in the church to pray for you. You cannot imagine what an amazing difference He will make in your life.

What happens when we are filled with the Holy Spirit?

1 We know they are God's children.

I know, what you are thinking, we already know we are God's children when we get saved. Yes, that is true, we know it in our minds. But when the Holy Spirit dwells

within us that, "The Spirit himself testifies with our spirit that we are God's children." (Romans 14:16")
We don't just know it now, we know it in our heads, our hearts and in our spirits. In other words, we are certain!

2 We understand Spiritual things

If you remember, before we became Christians, our spirits were dead in our sin. So, it stands to reason that we couldn't understand spiritual things. Now that we have the Holy Spirit living in us and our spirits our now alive in Christ Jesus, we begin to see thing in a completely different light. Once we could only see things from a worldly point of view, now we have the enlightenment of the Holy Spirit within us. It doesn't happen all at once, we have so many things to **un**learn. But as we spend time in prayer with the Lord we will grow in spiritual understanding.

3 We have insight into the Scriptures

John 14:26 tells us, "Jesus said: But the Advocate, the Holy Spirit, whom the Father will send in my name, will teach you all things and will remind you of everything I have said to you."

I must confess, before I became a Christian, the Bible did not make any sense to me at all. I thought it was boring and confusing. When I became a Christian, it suddenly began to make sense.

I remember saying on the night I got saved, "I still don't believe in the virgin birth."
That same week I was reading the Bible and read the part about Mary when the angel told Her she was going to have child even though she was a virgin and suddenly

it made sense to me. Of course, Jesus was the son of God; no man could possibly be His father. I believe that it was the Holy Spirit revealed that to me.

The more I read the Bible, the more the Holy Spirit reveals to me, and the more He reveals to me the more interesting the Bible becomes. Of course, some parts are still hard to understand, so it is always best to pray for the Lord to make clear what He is trying to teach you through His Word.

And just a word of encouragement, don't be misled into thinking that some parts of the Bible don't count. 2 Timothy 3:16-17 says, "All Scripture is God-breathed and is useful for teaching, rebuking, correcting, and training in righteousness, so that the servant of God may be thoroughly equipped for every good work".

Yes, all of God's word is there for our benefit, even the difficult bits, so let's not ignore them but pray that the Holy Spirit will help us to understand them. There is such a wealth of Godly teaching in the Bible we need all of it.

4 We are helped to pray

Let's be honest, it can be difficult to pray at times, can't it? We get distracted
Or we just can't think of anything to say. This is what Paul wrote about it in Romans 8:26-28,
"In the same way, the Spirit helps us in our weakness. We do not know what we ought to pray for, but the Spirit himself intercedes for us through wordless groans. And he who searches our hearts knows the mind of the Spirit, because the Spirit intercedes for God's people in accordance with the will of God.

in mind, be alert and always keep on praying for all the Lord's people."

Remember, we have the Holy Spirit in us, and He can use our prayers to God's glory. As we wait upon Him, He can direct our thoughts to pray what He wants us to pray.

Sometimes, if we have the Gift of tongues, (we will talk more about that later) then we can pray in tongues, and even though we don't know what we are saying, the Holy Spirit uses those words we pray to pray through us to God the Father. And sometimes it is just Good to wait upon the Holy Spirit silently, allowing Him to minister to us and strengthen our walk with God.

5 We live to please God

Romans 8:5-10 says:
"Those who live according to the flesh have their minds set on what the flesh desires."

That used to be us. We were only interested in things of the flesh; we knew nothing about Spiritual matters, and we didn't want to know. And later in the same verses it says,
"The mind governed by the flesh is death,"

and also,
"The mind governed by the flesh is hostile to God; it does not submit to God's law, nor can it do so. Those who are in the realm of the flesh cannot please God."

Oh dear what a mess we were in. But isn't God wonderful? He wanted so much better for us. By His Holy Spirit He convicted us our sin and we gave our lives to Jesus. That was the first thing we did that pleased Him. Then the Holy Spirit got to work on us, and if we are not stubborn, and live in accordance with the Holy Spirit, we have our, minds set on what the Holy Spirit desires. And the mind governed by the Holy Spirit is life and peace.

A word of warning to all of us, if we don't live the life that God wants us to and ignore the leading of the Holy Spirit, not only are we not pleasing God, but we are also sacrificing our own peace and joy. But having said that I am sure that as Spirit filled Christians, we all want to please God. The Holy Spirit helps to do that.

6 We become more like Jesus

We will soon be reading about the fruit of the Holy Spirit in detail, *"But the fruit of the Spirit is love, joy, peace, patience, kindness, goodness, faithfulness, gentleness, and self-control. Against such things there is no law.* **"Galatians 5:22-23**

This beautiful fruit is the very Character of Jesus and it what the Holy Spirit wants to impart into our lives. What a privilege it is that the God of creation, The Lord of Heaven and Earth, is so interested in us that He patiently works on our spirit with His Spirit to make such a difference in our lives. Let us not kick against the goads, but say, "Yes Lord, make me more like Christ."

How does the Holy Spirit help the Church as a body?

To be in a Spirit filled Church is the most amazing, exciting places on Earth to be. You feel love as soon as you enter the building, and the atmosphere is vibrant with His presence. There is a unity among the people there that you don't feel elsewhere.

1 Corinthians 12:12-13 says:
"Just as a body, though one, has many parts, but all its many parts form one body, so it is with Christ. For we were all baptized by[a] one Spirit so as to form one body—whether Jews or Gentiles, slave or free —and we were all given the one Spirit to drink."

The preaching will be anointed with power, with conviction, with encouragement and with grace.

The very presence of the Holy Spirit Flowing through the congregation causes everyone to want to praise Jesus with all our hearts, and worship flows freely as we focus on Jesus and although our styles of worship might be completely different, it will all unite into something beautiful.

Some may pray out loud, some quietly in their hearts. Someone may prophecy; someone may give a message in tongues while someone else might share what the message means.

Wonderful things happen in a Spirit filled meeting, very often people receive the calling to the ministry that God wants them to do, "some to be apostles, some to be teachers, some to be pastors." (Ephesians 4:11) and so many other ministries. Some very humble but important, some that may take you across the world such as missionaries.

I believe everybody in the church has a ministry and if we ask the Lord, He will reveal to us what it is. My first ministry was handing out hymn books to people as they came into church; my second one was cleaning the church, and I delighted in doing them because I was doing something useful in the House of God.

A Spirit filled Church wants to reach out with the Gospel and the Holy Spirit gives them the ability and boldness to do it.

Acts 1:8 says:
Jesus said: "But you will receive power when the Holy Spirit comes on you; and you will be my witnesses in Jerusalem, and in all Judea and Samaria, and to the ends of the earth."
And Acts 4-31 says:
"After they prayed, the place where they were meeting was shaken. And they were all filled with the Holy Spirit and spoke the word of God boldly."

To the Church that is made up of Spirit filled Christians, the Holy Spirit will direct them into the outreach that He want them to do, as individuals and as a body.

Hallelujah! Let's give Jesus all the Glory!

Also, when the Holy Spirit comes, He comes with Spiritual gifts for God's people.

So, let's talk about

The Gifts of the Holy Spirit

What are the gifts the Holy Spirit Brings?

They are many and varied. Some are mentioned directly...

Romans 12:6-8 says:
"We have different gifts, according to the grace given to each of us. If your gift is prophesying, then prophesy in accordance with your faith; if it is serving, then serve; if it is teaching, then teach; if it is to encourage, then give encouragement; if it is giving, then give generously; if it is to lead, do it diligently; if it is to show mercy, do it cheerfully."

And 1 Corinthians 12:7-10
"Now to each one the manifestation of the Spirit is given for the common good. To one there is given through the Spirit a message of wisdom, to another a message of knowledge by means of the same Spirit, to another faith by the same Spirit, to another gifts of healing by that one Spirit, to another miraculous powers, to another prophecy, to another distinguishing between spirits, to another speaking in different kinds of tongues, and to still another the interpretation of tongues."

1 Corinthians 12: 28 tells us how the Lord will direct us into ministries by His Holy Spirit.
"And God has placed in the church first of all apostles, second prophets, third teachers, then miracles, then gifts of healing, of helping, of guidance, and of different kinds of tongues."

Are there gifts for all God's people?

Yes, there are, including you and I. the Bible teaches us that **Everyone has at least one gift**
1 Corinthians 12:7
"Now to each one the manifestation of the Spirit is given for the common good."
Notice that, "each one", in other words all of us.

To confirm that Romans 12:4-6 says,
"For just as each of us has one body with many members, and these members do not all have the same function, so in Christ we, though many, form one body, and each member belongs to all the others. We have different gifts, according to the grace given to each of us. If your gift is prophesying, then prophesy in accordance with your faith.
God gives His gifts as He decides.

1 Corinthians 12:4-6 says:
"There are different kinds of gifts, but the same Spirit distributes them. There are different kinds of service, but the same Lord. There are different kinds of working, but in all of them and in everyone it is the same God at work."

I am very glad that God decides which gift to each of us. It takes the responsibility away from us wondering which gift we would like. The wonderful thing is that God knows which gift suits us best and He also knows how to organise His Church best. The Lord knows that **Every member in the Church is different.**

1 Corinthians 12:14-20

"Even so the body is not made up of one part but of many. Now if the foot should say, "Because I am not a hand, I do not belong to the body," it would not for that reason stop being part of the body. And if the ear should say, "Because I am not an eye, I do not belong to the body," it would not for that reason stop being part of the body. If the whole body were an eye, where would the sense of hearing be? If the whole body were an ear, where would the sense of smell be? But in fact, God has placed the parts in the body, every one of them, just as he wanted them to be. If they were all one part, where would the body be? As it is, there are many parts, but one body."

Isn't it clever how Paul compared the Church, to the human body? It helps us to make sense of why God distributes the gifts the way He does. Since Jesus went back to Heaven, the Bible refers to the Church as the "body of Christ." (1Corinthians 12:27) and as the body of Christ **we are All are needed with our own Spiritual gift.**

1 Corinthians 12:21-22
"The eye cannot say to the hand, "I don't need you!" And the head cannot say to the feet, "I don't need you!" On the contrary, those parts of the body that seem to be weaker are indispensable."

And if you need more convincing, it says in
1 Corinthians 12;27. "Now you are the body of Christ, and each one of you is a part of it."

Our Spiritual gifts have two purposes
Firstly, of course they are to build us up as individuals; to help us to live a victorious Christian life. But secondly, and just as importantly, we should seek to use the gifts to help the church to grow spiritually.

1 Corinthians 14:12 encourages us with this when it says, "Since you are eager for gifts of the Spirit, try to excel in those that build up the church." When we say "the church" here we are not talking about a building or a group of nameless people. We are talking about brothers and sisters all brought together by our love for the Lord and His Love for us. We are meeting together with people we love.

In John 13:34 Jesus said, "A new commandment I give unto you, that you love one another as I have loved you."

Love needs to be the catalyst that inspires us to build each other up. 1 Corinthians 12:31-13:8 says, "And yet I will show you the most excellent way. If I speak in the tongues of men or of angels, but do not have love, I am only a resounding gong or a clanging cymbal. If I have the gift of prophecy and can fathom all mysteries and all knowledge, and if I have a faith that can move mountains, but do not have love, I am nothing. If I give all I possess to the poor and give over my body to hardship that I may boast but do not have love, I gain nothing. Love is patient, love is kind. It does not envy, it does not boast, it is not proud. It does not dishonour others, it is not self-seeking, it is not easily angered, it keeps no record of wrongs. Love does not delight in evil but rejoices with the truth. It always protects, always trusts, always hopes, always perseveres. Love never fails."

Isn't that why we want the gifts of the Spirit? That we might glorify God and build up His Church. That is why it says in 1Corinthians 14:1,
"Follow the way of love and eagerly desire gifts of the Spirit."

How are God's gifts used?

What ever gift the Lord has given us we should use it with humility, with order, with wisdom - not selfishly.

1Peter 4:10-11 says, "Each of you should use whatever gift you have received to serve others, as faithful stewards of God's grace in its various forms. If anyone speaks, they should do so as one who speaks the very words of God. If anyone serves, they should do so with the strength God provides, so that in all things God may be praised through Jesus Christ. To him be the glory and the power for ever and ever. Amen."

That brings us down to Earth a bit doesn't it" it is not a contest to see who has got the best gift, We need to use our gifts sensitively, not to do so would not bring glory to God.

1 Corinthians 14:26-33.40 says,
"What then shall we say, brothers and sisters? When you come together, each of you has a hymn, or a word of instruction, a revelation, a tongue or an interpretation. Everything must be done so that the church may be built up."

Now what are these precious gifts we are talking about? Let's read *1 Corinthians 12:7-11*

"But the manifestation of the Spirit is given to each one for the profit of all: for to one is given the word of wisdom through the Spirit, to another the word of knowledge through the same Spirit, to another faith by

the same Spirit, to another gifts of healings by the same Spirit, to another the working of miracles, to another prophecy, to another discerning of spirits, to another different kinds of tongues, to another the interpretation of tongues. But one and the same Spirit works all these things, distributing to each one individually as He will."

Now that we know them let us look at each gift in turn.

1. The Word of Knowledge

.

The Word of Knowledge is simply the Holy Spirit transmitting His specific knowledge to you on something that you would have no ability or means to be able to know about with your own limited intelligence and knowledge levels. It is supernatural knowledge and insight being given directly to you by the Holy Spirit Himself, not by your own mind or your own intelligence levels.

This gift is very often used in church. Someone may stand up and say something like, "the Lord has said to me that someone here has a back problem, and He is going to heal it."

The person giving this word of knowledge did not already know about the persons back, he or she are just
Sharing what the Lord has said to them, but the person with the bad back have their faith built up, knowing God is going to heal them.

Of course, words of knowledge can be about anything, not just healing, but whatever the word is it will be encouraging. When words of knowledge are shared, they are to build the faith of the people in the church, never to reveal peoples' secrets or embarrass people.

2. The Word of Wisdom

This next gift will at times work in conjunction with the word of knowledge. Sometimes all you need is a direct word of knowledge from the Holy Spirit, and it will completely solve the problem or dilemma you are dealing with.

However, there will be other times that a word of knowledge will not be quite enough to solve the problem. This is where you will now need a word of wisdom. A word of wisdom will give you the ability to be able to properly apply the knowledge that you may already have on a particular situation.

There is a big difference between knowledge, and wisdom. For instance, you may have the knowledge of how to play the bagpipes, but wisdom tell you not to play them at 3am when everyone is asleep!

Proverbs 9:10 says, "The (reverent) Fear of the Lord is the beginning of Wisdom."

In other words, when we first realise that we are lost sinners in need of salvation, and we give our hearts to Jesus, we are finally beginning to gain wisdom. The longer we are in the Lord and the more we surrender our lives to Him the greater our wisdom grows.
The more we read His word the more our wisdom grows, until finally we the only true wisdom is found in God, and we no longer lean on our own understanding.
Solomon was the wisest man ever, why, because he asked God for wisdom. He wasn't too proud to admit his own wisdom wasn't enough for him to be a good king of Israel. When we stop being wise in our own eyes, and we start to trust in the Lord with all our hearts, (Proverbs 3:5) we are putting ourselves in the right position to receive the true wisdom that the Holy Spirit Brings.

We all need words of wisdom from the Holy Spirit in our daily life, so we will know how to handle more complex types of problems or issues that can occur at a moment's notice in our daily lives.

Here are some specific examples where we could receive words of wisdom direct from the Holy Spirit:

1. Your boss has just given you a new tough assignment and you are not sure on how to get the job properly done.
You will now need God's knowledge and wisdom on how to get this new assignment successfully completed.
2. Your finances have spiralled out of control, and you will now need God's guidance and wisdom on how to keep yourself out of bankruptcy.

3. You have just been named in an unjust lawsuit and you will now need God's wisdom on how to properly handle it.

As you can see, there are literally an infinite number of possibilities where you will need God's wisdom to get you safely though the problem or dilemma you are now having to face.

Again, since our own human intelligence is so imperfect and so limited in its ability to apply real wisdom to handle and solve some of life's real tough problems, we all need the wisdom of God flowing through our lives on a regular basis so we can handle and overcome many of life's adversities that can get thrown our way at any time.

3. The Gift of Prophecy

"I would like every one of you to speak in tongues, but I

would rather have you prophesy. The one who prophesies is greater than the one who speaks in tongues (unless someone interprets,) so that the church may be edified." (1 Corinthians 14:5)

I think it is wonderful be able to receive a direct, clear, prophetic Word from the Lord to be able to give to someone else in order to help edify and build them up, or to help them out with something specific they may be dealing with, with you being the **actual messenger** of that prophetic word to that someone.

The gift of prophesy is normally used in Church meetings. Sometimes to encourage the preacher that he is preaching what God wants them to. For instance, if the preacher has prepared a sermon about healing and then one of the congregation who has no idea what he is going to preach about, speaks out with a word from the Lord about healing. Imagine how encouraging that is to the preacher that he or she are on the right track with their sermon.

When someone speaks out with the prophetic word the Lord has given to them, they do it in faith. They have no idea if anyone will pick up on it, and sometimes they never find out, but sometimes an individual in the congregation will realise that word was for them, to help them.
Many times, prophecy is also used to help confirm what has already been given to the person earlier on by the Lord. Sometimes God will confirm for you what He has already told you earlier so you will know that it really was Him all along giving you that specific message. And one of the ways that He can confirm a previous message that He has already given you is by giving you a direct prophecy through another believer.

Prophecies from the Lord can cover an extremely wide range of situations and issues, covering everything from predicting future events like they use to do in the Old Testament, to giving someone counsel, encouragement, confirmation, instruction, and possible correction when it may be needed.

Also, all prophecy needs to be properly tested, as the Bible tells us that there will always be false prophets walking among us, along with the possibility of well-meaning believers prophesying out of their own imaginations. Here is the verse giving us this direct warning:
"Do not quench the Spirit. Do not despise prophecies. Test all things; hold fast what is good." (1 Thessalonians 5:19-21)

All prophecy always needs to line up with Scripture. If it does not, it should be immediately rejected. God will never go against His own Word when delivering a prophetic word to someone.

Again, any believer can be used by the Lord in this gift.

The Bible tells us that in the latter days God will be pouring out His Holy Spirit upon all flesh, (Joel 2:28) and when He does, it says our sons and daughters will be prophesying. This means that there are going to be many believers who are going to be getting this gift manifesting through them with a lot of frequency in the coming years.

When Paul says to **"desire earnestly to prophesy"** and to **"desire spiritual gifts, but especially that you may prophesy,"** you know that this is something that the Lord would really like to do more of with His children.

Again, if you would like the Lord to manifest this gift through you so that you can be a direct messenger for Him to someone else, just go to Him in prayer and tell Him that you would be more than happy to be a willing and yielded vessel for Him to manifest this particular gift through if He would like to do so. And then keep your radars up, always being open and sensitive to the Holy Spirit if He will want to start manifesting this gift through you so He can use it to help build others up and bring some comfort, joy, peace, or direction into their lives.

4. The Gift of Faith

This next gift, the gift of faith, is faith that comes directly from the Holy Spirit.

The Bible tells us that we all have a certain measure of faith that has already been given to us by the Lord. God has to give each person a certain measure of faith or we would not be able to get saved, as the Bible tells us that we are saved by **"faith"** through grace. And then over the course of our walks with the Lord, our faith will continue to grow to higher levels as we continue to draw closer to the Lord in our own personal relationship with Him and increase our knowledge levels about Him through the study of Scripture.

However, there will be times that our own levels of faith in the Lord will not be enough to get the job done with what He may be asking us to do for Him. Here is an example:

In 1 Kings 17, we read the story of Elijah. He commanded it not to rain, and for three and a half years it did not rain. God told Elijah to say it would not rain. There is no way on Earth that in the strength of our own faith we could do that, it was the special **gift of faith** working in Elijah that allowed him to move in such power.

Three and a half years later the Lord told Elijah to pray that it would rain. In obedience Elijah prayed, and nothing happened! So, did he give up praying? No! He kept on praying. After awhile his servant who had been watching the empty skies for something to happen, said to Elijah, "I can see a cloud about the size of a man's hand."
To which Elijah replied, "I hear the sound of an abundance of rain." (1Kings 18:41).

He told the king who was up the mountain where he was praying to get down the mountain as quick as possible before he was caught in the deluge to come!

Could anyone have such faith to pray such things and expect the to happen? I don't think so, it is a case of the **gift of faith** at work. When his servant saw the tiny cloud, Elijah couldn't hear anything with his physical ears, or see anything with his physical eyes, it was through the ears and eyes of faith he new these things.

The Holy Spirit is still dispensing the Gift of faith today and we don't have to be anyone in particular to receive. We just need to be open to God and be ready to be used by him.

Sometimes God may ask you to do something that will be out of your comfort zone. Fear and panic will immediately set in because you have never done what He is now asking you to do.

When this should ever happen to you, just ask the Holy Spirit to manifest His faith, courage, and boldness up in you so you will have His faith, strength, and courage to do what God is asking you to do for Him. But always remember, He will **never** ask you to do something that is not in line with His word, the Bible.

5. The Gifts of Healings

At any time, the Holy Spirit can manifest this special gift through any believer so that He can then heal someone of any kind of disease, illness, or sickness. You do not have to have the gift of healing as any kind of a full- time ministry to be able to have the Holy Spirit do this through you. Again, this can literally happen to any single believer at any time with the Lord.

However, some people seem to move in this ministry more often than other. Evangelists and preachers of the Gospel, for instance seem to very often have the gift of healings. In Matthew 10 Jesus sent out the disciples to preach the Gospel, but before he did, he equipped them. In verse one it says, "He gave them authority to drive out impure spirits and to heal every disease and sickness." And in Mark 16 we read that signs always followed the preaching of the Gospel.

Is the gift of healings still available today? Yes, it is. But like all the gifts, we need to want it, to pray for the Lord to bestow the gift upon us, and then to be bold and step out in faith to use the gift. How do we know if we have the gift? Simply by being bold enough to pray for people. Not just in our quiet times but when we are with them. The Bible tells us to "Lay hands on the sick and they shall recover." (Mark 16:18). So let's be obedient so that we can see more people healed.

I have also noticed that when people move in the gift of healings they very often also work in the gift of knowledge. For instance, the person with this gift may say something like, "I feel that somebody here has bad pain in their neck, if that is you, please come forward so I can pray for you."
In this way God is telling that person He wants to heal them, but it is up to the person concerned to respond in

faith, to receive their healing.

Also notice that the wording being used in this verse is that this is the **"gifts"** of healing. The word **"gifts"** is plural, which means there are different kinds of healings the Lord will want to do.

People who walk with this kind of anointing on a regular basis have found out is that some people will be more gifted and anointed in some areas than they will be in other areas.

 For instance, some people may have more success with healing bad back cases, where another may have a stronger anointing to heal cancer cases. In other words, the Lord will sometimes specialize on the kinds of healings He will want to do through an individual believer.

It also means that not all the people we pray for will be healed. That is why it says **"gifts"**. Each time God heals someone it is a gift.
Nobody knows why God does not heal everyone, only God knows that.

An American lady evangelist called Kathryn Kuhlman who ministered from the 1940s to the 1970s, had an amazing healing ministry. She also worked in words of knowledge as mentioned above. So successful was her ministry that hospitals used to take coach loads of people to her meetings, all in the hope of receiving a miraculous healing from the Lord. But although many people were healed, not everyone was.

Did the fact that not everyone as healed stop her praying for others? Of course not! And as a result, many, many people received their miraculous healing from the Lord.

Kathryn could not understand why God chose to heal some but not others and she once remarked, "When I get to Heaven the first question, I am going to ask the Lord is why everyone wasn't healed." So let us not be discouraged if not everyone we pray for is healed, let us just keep praying for them

If you want to be used in the gift of healing it is good to read as many scriptures on healing as you can that are mentioned in the Bible as it will show you that both God the Father in the Old Testament and Jesus Christ in the New Testament were constantly healing people on a regular basis. And if God does not change, and He is the same today as He was yesterday, then that means He still wants to continue His healing ministry in this day and age, and thus will anoint His believers with His healing power through the Holy Spirit.

6. The Working of Miracles

This next gift from the Holy Spirit is where you can get into some real heavy, jaw-dropping, knock-your-socks off type of supernatural activity from Him.

Some of the different Bible Dictionaries describe the word miracle as the following:

· **An intervention in the natural universe by God**
· **A phenomenon that transcends natural laws.**
· **A divine act by which God reveals Himself to people.**
·

Good examples of actual miracles from the Bible are the

following:
1. **Jesus and the apostles healing and casting demons out of people.**
2. **Jesus turning water into wine at the wedding of Cana.**
3. **Jesus feeding 5000 people by multiplying 5 loaves of bread and two fish.**
4. **God parting the Red Sea for Moses and the children of Israel.**
5. **Daniel not being eaten by the lions in the lion's den.**
6. **Peter walking on water.**

If you study the Bible very carefully from start to finish, it is literally one miracle after another with both God the Father and Jesus Christ. Our God is a miracle-working God and He still loves to do them for His people.

The Bible says that God does not change, and if both Him and Jesus were constantly doing miracles in both the Old and New Testament, then God will also be wanting to do miracles in our day and age. And with this specific gift being listed as one of the gifts of the Holy Spirit, then you know that God is trying to tell all of us that He still wants to do them, even in these sceptical times that we are now currently living in.

Of course, every healing that the Lord does is a miracle really, but very often sceptics can call these healings a coincidence and that the person would have recovered. We call it a miracle when there is no doubt that it is something performed by God.

For instance, even in this day and age I have heard of people being raised from the dead. Another wonderful testimony I heard was a man being prayed for, for something I don't remember, but after he had been prayed for, he rushed to the evangelist who had prayed for him in a state shock and happy amazement. He hadn't told the evangelist that he had a glass eye, but while the evangelist was praying, the Lord turned his glass ye into a real flesh and blood eye that could see! Nobody could deny that that was a miracle.

There are a great deal of miracles happening around the world and not all of them are healing miracles. Such as the lady who drove her car for about 50 miles to an important meeting, only to be, when she got there, that the fuel line was not connected!

Miracles encourage faith, and reveal God's power to believers and unbelievers alike, and fulfil God will.

God loves to perform miracles, and I believe God can perform miracles for everyone and can perform them **through** anyone. So why not me? Why not you? I don't mind who God uses, I just want to see Him move in a mighty way, don't you? Let's pray that God glorifies His name in this way.

7. The Discerning of spirits

This next gift is one that is a totally Spiritual one. It is not seen with the eye or felt physically. It is a revelation to our spirit from the Holy Spirit.

Sometimes something can really seem like a really good idea or blessing from God but is in fact the devil trying to lead us astray.

A good example of that is what happened to Johnny Cash the country and western singer when he was young. He was working hard going from town to town singing his songs and he got totally exhausted. The someone introduced him to drugs to keep him awake. (uppers). Johnny felt so good when he started taking them that he thought they were a gift from God. How wrong he was! The trouble was he was to wide awake to sleep, so he started taking downers to relax him. Before he knew it he was totally addicted. It was years before, with help he got free.

I think you will agree that drugs that seemed so good at first were a trap set by the devil to ensnare him.

In the 1970s a man named Jim Jones who started off as a Christian preacher ended up starting a cult. So charismatic a man was he that his followers hung onto his every word. So much so that when his teachings turned away from the Bible, they still followed him. His followers were completely miss led and the tragedy was that in 1978 he caused them all to commit suicide.

If any of his followers had discernment of the spirits, they would have realized that Jim Jones had turned away from

God and was preaching the lies of Satan.

I once met a man who seemed very nice and friendly and there was nothing apparently wrong with him, but I had feeling in my heart that there was some very wrong about him. Only later did I find out that he was a practicing witch who worshipped the devil. I believe it was the Holy Spirit that gave me that discernment.

One way we can all discern if something is not of God is by checking it against the Bible. If it doesn't agree with the Bible, it is not of God. But the Gift of discernment goes further than that.

What happens in this gift is that the Holy Spirit will give you supernatural discernment, insight, and knowledge. Many of the times, this gift will be used to fully expose what is really going on and operating behind the scenes with someone.

There are the types of Spirit:
The human spirit (our own thoughts and Feelings)
Demonic spirits
And the Holy Spirit

Here is how this gift will come into play with each one of these kinds of spirits.

a) Human Spirits – in addition to angels and demonic spirits, the first kind of spirit this gift is referring to is just our own human spirits. For instance, someone could have a bad spirit of pride on them. It will not be a demonic spirit giving this person this kind of bad pride, it will just be his own natural spirit, as we are all totally capable of having bad kinds of spirits build up in our systems without the help of any kind of demonic spirits, since we have already been born into this world as corrupt sinners.

It is good when the Holy Spirit reveal to us some of the real bad apples that are out there, especially those of the criminal type such as money scammers and swindlers. None of us want to be duped, so it is good idea for all of us to pray for discernment in these matters.

Unfortunately, the human spirit is very often at work in the church. What seem like "good ideas" are not always "God ideas". It is so important not to get carried away with our own ideas, but to always ask for Holy Spirit discernment when making plans and decisions concerning church matters.

Sometimes we wonder why the things we are doing for God are not going right and ending in failure. It is usually because we never checked with God first. It might take time to develop the gift of discernment, but it something we need to succeed in the Lord.

B) demonic spirits
Some Christians get nervous or afraid at the mention of demonic forces but there is no need to be. James 2:19 tells us that demons tremble at the name of Jesus.
As born -again Christians we have complete dominion over evil spirits because we have Jesus and the Holy Spirit in us.

Others seem to see demons in everything that goes wrong. You have probably heard people say something like, "the devil was having a go at me this morning. First my bus was late, then I go splashed by a car and was soaking wet!"

The bus was probably late because of a traffic jam and the car driver that splashed you was being driven by a person not the devil. So, let's get real when we are talking about these things.

Sadly, some people have lived in sin so long that they have allowed demonic spirits to come and dwell within them. Since some demons are very good at hiding on the inside of someone once they enter in, God needs to activate this gift through some of His own so they can detect when a demon is on the inside of someone and expose its presence.

Once the demon has been exposed, then you can set the person up for a deliverance. But the first thing to be able to do is to discern and detect that the demons are already on the inside of that person in the first place.

People who have the gift of discernment of spirits sometimes actually see the demonic spirits. Others just sense their presence.

Isn't it wonderful that God loves us so much that He wants to bless us with such a wonderful gift? And although some people move in this gift more than others it is available to us all as we learn to Listen to the Holy Spirit's leading. Don't be misled, if something doesn't agree with the Bible, no matter how good an idea it seems, it isn't from the Holy Spirit.

c) **The Holy Spirit**

The Holy Spirit is the one we all want to be sensitive to, isn't He? He is the one who will lead us into all truths. He is the one who points us to Jesus. He is the one who will empower us to do the will of God.

In Proverbs 3 :5 we read, "Trust in the Lord with all your heart and lean not on your own understanding." And in verse 7 it says, "Be not wise in your own eyes." This is how we must be to be open to the Holy Spirit. Completely trusting in Him.

Get to know your Bible. It is imperative that we read our Bibles, or we can't recognise the leading of God's Spirit. The Holy Spirit will never tell us to do anything that goes against the teaching of God Word, so no matter how good an idea something might seem, if it doesn't line up with the Bible it is not from the Holy Spirit.

On the other hand, if the Holy Spirit lays something on your heart that **does** line up with Bible, no matter how difficult it may seem to you, go with it. When the Lord calls you to do something, run with it. Whom the Lord calls He also equips.

If You feel God is calling you to do something, pray about it. Ask Him to reassure you that the idea is from and not yourself. Wait on God prayerfully, and when you know that you know it is of Him, run with it. God **will** strengthen you for the road ahead.

8. Different Kinds of Tongues

The gift of tongues is simply the Holy Spirit giving you the supernatural ability to speak in a foreign tongue that you have no knowledge or ability to speak out on your own.

There are two types of tongues He can give you. One is a tongue of this Earth. For instance, if your native language is English, then He can give you the ability to speak in Chinese, Japanese, or Spanish, etc.

The other type of tongue that He can give you is a tongue direct from heaven, a heavenly language that is not of this earth. The Bible tells us in 1 Corinthians 13 that there are, **"tongues of angels."**

But in either event, it will be a foreign language that you will not be able to speak out on your own, and only the Holy Spirit's supernatural transmission of this language out of your spirit will give you the ability to be able to speak this language out. And whatever tongue the Holy Spirit will give you, you will be able to use it 24/7, whenever you want. It will be your own personal, private, prayer language between you and the Lord.

The only problem with this gift is that for the most part, you will never know or understand what you are praying about when you go into this gift.

The Bible tells us that we will be speaking out **"mysteries,"** and only God the Father and the Holy Spirit will be knowing exactly what the prayer will be about on any given occasion when you are actually doing it.

So, if we will not know exactly what we are praying about when using this gift, then why would God even want us to have this kind of a gift in the first place?

I believe the reason is in the verse where it says that sometimes we will not know how to pray as we ought to. Sometimes we will not be able to find the right words to use in our own personal prayers to the Lord due to our own natural imperfections in being able to properly communicate with Him.

Here is the verse that will show us that sometimes we will not know how to pray as we ought, and that we all need the Holy Spirit to come and help us out in our own personal prayer life with God the Father:

Romans 8:26 says: "Likewise, the Spirit also helps in our weaknesses. For we do not know what we should pray for as we ought, but the Spirit Himself makes intercession for us with groanings which cannot be uttered."

The Holy Spirit is the Master when it comes to praying to God the Father and as such, He is allowing us to have direct access into His own personal prayer life with God the Father. In other words, He is asking us to play a part of and to share with Him on His own direct, personal prayers to God the Father.

Even though you will not know what you are praying about when you do go into your gift of tongues, at least you will have the honour and privilege of being able to pray direct to God the Father with the Holy Spirit. And since the Holy Spirit knows how to present a perfect prayer to God the Father, then you can actually play a part in that perfect prayer to God the Father.

Another reason that you will want this gift is for emergency situations. I have heard of many occasions where the Holy Spirit will suddenly prompt someone to start praying in tongues, and then later on that person finds out that the prayer they were just doing in tongues was just used to change someone's circumstances.

For the most part, the gift of tongues will be used as your own personal, private, prayer language between you and the Lord.

If you are praying in tongues in church, sometimes something happens. You may be praying quietly in tongues, just between you and God, and then the Holy Spirit moves in a wonderful way, and suddenly you, or somebody else start to speak loudly in tongues. This is called, "giving a word in tongues." When that happens, then usually someone else will have the interpretation of that tongue. This is another way of giving a prophecy as we talked about earlier.

With our inability to be perfect prayer warriors with God

the Father, I believe this is one gift that God would like all of His children to have. When you find yourself wanting to pray to God, but you find yourself falling short in how you want to pray or what you want to pray about, you can just go into your gift of tongues with the Holy Spirit and then end up giving God a perfect prayer, since the prayer will be coming direct from the Holy Spirit Himself.

This a very powerful prayer tool to have in your own arsenal since you are opening yourself up direct to the Holy Spirit and His ability to perfectly pray to God the Father. You are joining forces with the third Person of the Trinity who is God and Lord Himself, who is the Master Intercessor with God the Father.

Just meditate on this mind-blowing reality, and then see think about asking God the Father to release this powerful gift to you through the Holy Spirit.

9 the interpretation of tongues

This next gift is where the Holy Spirit will give you the interpretation of the tongues that you have either spoken yourself or when they spoken by someone else in a church setting.

Here are the two main verses telling you where the gift of

interpretation will come into play with the gift of tongues:

1. "If anyone speaks in a tongue, let there be two or at the most three, each in turn, and let one interpret. But if there is no interpreter, let him keep silent in church, and let him speak to himself and to God." **(1 Corinthians 14: 27-28)**

2. "Therefore let him who speaks in a tongue pray that he may interpret. For if I pray in a tongue, my spirit prays, but my understanding is unfruitful." **(1 Corinthians 14:13-14)**

 The first verse has to do with others interpreting a tongue when it is done in a church service. The second verse is showing you that the Holy Spirit can give you the interpretation of your own tongue as you are praying in it all by yourself.

Again, another very powerful gift that you can ask to receive from the Lord.

Conclusion

Just stop and think about what all nine of these gifts from the Holy Spirit are really about. We are talking about God Almighty Himself coming down and manifesting a part of Himself through these nine gifts, since God, Jesus, and the Holy Spirit are perfectly one with one another in the Divine Trinity.

With every single one of these nine gifts being direct, miraculous manifestations from the Holy Spirit, when we start to move in them, we are going deeper into a spiritual walk with the Lord. And that is exactly what God is asking all of us to do with these nine special gifts.

When the apostle Paul, tells us to "desire earnestly" these spiritual gifts and not to be afraid to try and stir these gifts up with the Lord, then you know God the Father wants us to move in these wonderful gifts.

In 1 Corinthians 12:31 it says, "Eagerly desire the greater gifts." But you might ask yourself, "Which are the greater gifts?"

I think the answer to that question is, whichever gift is needed at that time!

Although some people move in certain gifts more than others, that does not mean that **all** of us can't move in **all** of the gifts at some time or other in our lives as the need arises.

Just think how many more people you can help and save if you will allow the Holy Spirit to manifest some of these nine gifts through you when He desires. Each one of these nine gifts are major power gifts, and most of them are allowing the Lord to come in and manifest Himself to help someone else out.

Though Jesus is in heaven right now with His Father, we still have the Holy Spirit living on the inside of us. And through the Holy Spirit, both God the Father and Jesus Christ can still manifest Themselves into our daily lives and any situations that we will need Their help on.

Jesus is still in the rescue, help, and deliverance business – and if you will allow God to manifest these nine gifts through you, you yourself can become an actual partaker in some of his divine rescue, deliverance missions. You yourself can help carry on the divine supernatural ministry that Jesus left behind when He ascended to His Father.

Do you want to receive the gifts of the Holy Spirit? Do you want to be a vessel for Him to work through? Then surrender to Him now and seek Him with all your heart.

Jerimiah 29:15 says, "You will seek me and find me when you seek me with all your heart."

 The Lord wants His children to be filled with His Holy Spirit.God wants to lavish His gifts upon us. But God is the perfect gentleman, He will not come where He is not wanted. Nor will He bestow His gifts on those who are not ready for them.

Are you ready? Then seek Him with all your heart!

Let's talk about

But the fruit of the Spirit is love, joy, peace, patience, kindness, goodness, faithfulness, gentleness and self-control. Against such things there is no law.

Galatians 5:22-23

The Fruit of the Spirit -

The fruit of the Spirit is what the Holy Spirit wants to

produce in your life and in mine, in the life of all Christians. It is the character of Christ and the more we surrender to God the more fruit the Holy Spirit can produce in us.

When we first come to Christ, He accepts us just as we are, but He loves us too much to leave us like that. God has much better plans for us. We are God's representatives on Earth, and He wants people to see Christ in us. To do that God sends the Holy Spirit to help us to change our whole way of thinking and our attitude to life.

Once our lives were all about "me". But the Holy Spirit reveals to us that there is a better way, and He points us to Jesus and the more time we spend with Jesus, the more we want to be like Him.

But we can't do it on our we need the Holy Spirit to help us by bearing His Fruit in our lives.

We learn from scripture that these are not individual "fruits" from which we pick and choose. Rather, the fruit of the Spirit is one ninefold "fruit" that characterises all who truly walk in the Holy Spirit. Collectively, these are the fruits that all Christians should be producing in their new lives with Jesus Christ.

Fruit of the Spirit - The Nine Biblical Attributes

The fruit of the Spirit is what people should be able to see in a Christian's life. The more we surrender to Jesus the more this fruit should become apparent to people around us.

The Fruit of the Spirit is the very character of Jesus in us. God plants the Fruit of the Spirit in us when we become Christians, but it is up to us to nurture the Fruit, to make it grow by using it every day. So let us study and understand the attributes of the ninefold fruit that we might become more like Christ.

1 **Love** -

In Matthew 22:37-40 instructs His disciples on the importance of love.

 "Jesus replied: "Love the Lord your God with all your heart and with all your soul and with all your mind.' This is the first and greatest commandment. And the second is like it: 'Love your neighbour as yourself.' All the Law and the Prophets hang on these two commandments."

Once again in John 13:334-35 Jesus said,   "A new command I give you: love one another. As I have loved you, so you must love one another. By this all men will know that you are my disciples if you love one another."

Just in those couple of verses we can see how important that love is. Jesus thought it was so important that he actually **commanded** us to love one another.

Indeed if it wasn't for God's love we would be lost in sin, but as it says in John 3:16, "for God so **loved** the World, that He gave His only begotten Son that whosoever believes on Him should not perish but have everlasting life."

It was Christ's love that took Him to Calvary. It was Christ's love that held Him to the cross when He could have called ten thousand angels to come and set Him free. When Christ saw us lost in our wicked sinful state without a chance of going to Heaven, His love for us caused Him to give His life for us on that cruel cross to pay for our sins if we would just accept Him as our Lord and Saviour.

Love is the most powerful force in Heaven and Earth. The special supernatural love that come from God.

But how can we obey a commandment that tells us love one another? We love our families. We might be able to love our friends as long as they are nice to us; but in Matthew 5: 44 Jesus actually in tells us to love our enemies! That's a bit much isn't it? It sounds ridicules and impossible to do doesn't it? But let's face it, Christ died for us while we were yet sinners. (Romans 5:8) We were His enemies. We might have used His name as a swear word. But He loved us enough to die for us.

Perhaps we find the concept so difficult to imagine because we don't really understand what love is. When we realise that love isn't just an emotion or a feeling but a decision and an action, we start to get a better idea about the true meaning of the world "love."

1 Corinthians 13:4-8 tells us:
"Love is patient, love is kind. It does not envy, it does not boast, it is not proud. 5 It does not dishonour others, it is not self-seeking, it is not easily angered, it keeps no record of wrongs. 6 Love does not delight in evil but rejoices with the truth. 7 It always protects, always trusts, always hopes, always perseveres. Love never fails."

Do we want to obey Jesus' commandment to love each other? I do, but I don't think I can do it on my own. I think we all need the fruit of love to grow in our hearts. Then we can obey Jesus when He tell us to love our enemies, and do them good, and lend to them expecting nothing in return? (Luke 6:35)

Love seems to be the most over used word in the English language today, but it is just an empty word until we put it into practice in our hearts, in our minds and in our actions.

So let us examine ourselves today. Are we ready to love as Christ loves? It isn't easy but with a surrendered heart and the help of the Holy Spirit we can do it. There are times when we fail, but if we are serious in our commitment to obey this commandment, the lord will pick us up and help us to move in love. When we do we are opening up for the rest of the fruit to grow in our lives

2 Joy

Some people confuse the word joy with the word happiness, but they don't mean the same at all.

Happiness depends upon good things happening, whilst joy can be felt in the face of adversity, when nothing good is happening, because joy comes from a relationship with God. It is part of the fruit of the Spirit.

We can easily feel joyful wen we are at Church with our friends and loved ones singing God's praises. But how can we possibly find joy when we are on our own when everything seems to be going wrong and everything seems to be against us? It doesn't seem natural does it?

But the joy of the Lord isn't natural, it is Supernatural! It is from God. It is something we need to develop, and we do that by spending time in God's presence and by reading His word.

Joy isn't a commandment. It is not something we can just conjure up. Joy is part of the fruit of the Holy Spirit, and it needs to be nurtured.

When we realise God is completely in control of everything

that happens in our lives and that all things, even the bad things work together for our good (Romans 8:28). We start to get an idea that we can allow ourselves to be joyful.

Jesus is a wonderful example of this. In Hebrews 12:2 we are told " Jesus, the pioneer and perfecter of faith. endured the cross, scorning its shame, for the joy set before him, and sat down at the right hand of the throne of God." That joy, at such a horrible time, could only come through an intimate walk with God.

The closer we draw to God the greater our joy is, and we can say with the Psalmist, "The LORD is my strength and my shield; my heart trusts in him, and I am helped. My heart leaps for joy and I will give thanks to him in song." (Psalm 28:7)

Do you remember that absolute joy you felt when you first got saved? The thrill of being forgiven for all our sins and the realise just how much God loves us? Like the Psalmist we could say, "You turned my wailing into dancing; you removed my sackcloth and clothed me with joy," (Psalm 30 :11)
God wants us to feel that way all of the time. Sometimes it isn't easy to feel joy in bad situations, but if we remind ourselves that God is with us, walking hand in hand with us, we can stir up the fruit of joy in ourselves.

As we stir up this fruit we can feel a new strength come in to us to help us cope. As it says in Nehemiah 8:10, "the joy of the Lord is your strength."

3 **Peace** -

Before we can have the peace of God in our hearts, we first must make peace <u>with</u> God. We do that when we accept Jesus as our Lord and Saviour. Up until then we have just been living for ourselves in a world of rebellion to God, with our heavy load of sin stopping us from ever knowing God's peace. But on the day we get saved a wonderful thing happens. in Romans 5:1 it says, "Therefore, since we have been justified through faith, we have peace with God through our Lord Jesus Christ. "

It is then that we are able to receive a new kind of peace. Philippians 4:7 puts it this way. "And the peace of God, which transcends all understanding, will guard your hearts and your minds in Christ Jesus."

Or as Jesus says in John 14:27, "Peace I leave with you; my peace I give you. I do not give to you as the world gives. Do not let your hearts be troubled and do not be afraid."
 Romans 15:13 says," May the God of hope fill you with all joy and peace as you trust in him, so that you may overflow with hope by the power of the Holy Spirit. "

But how can we find peace in a sea of trouble? When we have so many things worrying us that we can't even sleep at night? Philippians 4:6-7 tells us how to do that, but it isn't always easy. We have to make up our minds to obey this scripture so we can have God's peace, we have to trust Him. The scripture says, "Do not be anxious about anything, but in every situation, by prayer and petition, with thanksgiving, present your requests to God And the peace of God, which transcends all understanding, will guard your hearts and your minds in Christ Jesus."

Let's be honest, we our only people and it is a human trait

to worry about things. But we are not on our own any longer. Now we belong to God! We have a Heavenly Father who loves us and promises to meet our every need, so we have to make a decision; do we carry on worrying, even though we know it doesn't change anything, or do we trust God who can, and is willing, to make everything work together for our good, as Romans 8:28 tells us.

Colossians 3:15 says "Let the peace of Christ rule in your hearts, since as members of one body you were called to peace."

That means we have a choice; we can accept the peace God offers or we can choose not to. I think that like me you will want to know God's peace, so let us allow the Holy Spirit to produce this wonderful fruit in our lives.

4 Longsuffering (patience) --

One definition of long suffering is to have the ability to suffer for a long time without giving up.

Some Christian really do have to suffer for their faith, even to the point of death sometimes. God really does help these amazing people. It says in Colossians 1:1, We are "being strengthened with all power according to his glorious might so that you may have great endurance and patience, " How amazing is that? God is there to strengthen us in our neediest times.

But for a lot of us long suffering means being patient. Patient with ourselves, patient with others and patient with our situations.

The Lord doesn't want us blowing our tops with people who annoy us. Ephesians 4:2 says,"Be completely humble and gentle; be patient, bearing with one another in love. "

And Proverbs 19:11 says "a man's wisdom gives him patience; it is to his glory to overlook an offense."

So what does that mean? It means it that it is isn't wise to keep losing our tempers. After all what does achieve? A bad atmosphere, tension and a breakdown in relationships. Not to mention how bad it makes us feel inside.

How much better to be patient with people. Try to see things from their point of view instead of flying off the handle.

If you struggle with impatience today, as all of us do at some time or other, then pause, take a breath, and ask the Lord to help you in this.

Sometimes we make the excuse that we can't help our lack of patience because we have a short fuse. But that is not true. We can make a decision to be patient and with the lord's help we can achieve it.

The number of stupid thinks I have done in my life and the number of times I have let God down; I am glad He has never lost His patience with me! No, every time I fall, he picks me up, brushes me down and sets me on my way again.

I want to have that kind of patience, don't you? So let us nurture that fruit in our lives.
As it says in Colossians 3:12, "Therefore, as God's chosen people, holy and dearly loved, clothe yourselves with compassion, kindness, humility, gentleness and **patience**."

4 **Kindness**

Galatians 6:7-8 says: "Do not be deceived: God is not to be mocked. Whatever a man sows, he will reap in return. The one who sows to please his flesh, from the flesh he will receive destruction; but the one who sows to please the Spirit, from the Spirit will reap eternal life."

From that reading alone we see the importance of being kind.
For a start, we should want to be kind for no other reason than it is the right thing to do. The Bible tells us to be kind and the Holy Spirit not only tells us to be kind but also gives us the ability to deny our old selfish natures, and to actually be kind.

The amazing thing is, God actually rewards us for our kindness. As we have just read, we reap what we sow, so if we sow kindness, we reap kindness. That is great, isn't it?

There is an old saying that "no good deed goes unpunished." That is rubbish and an excuse not to be kind to people. Of course, there are some ungrateful people, but one way or another we will receive kindness for the kindness we have shown.
 Proverbs 11:17 re-enforces this.
"A kind man (person) benefits himself, but a cruel man brings trouble on himself."

But even if no-one was ever kind to us, we should be kind anyway, because Jesus, the one gave His life for us on the cross, wants us too!

Colossians 3 :12 says,

"Therefore, as God's chosen people, holy and dearly loved, clothe yourselves with compassion and kindness."

And " 2 Corinthians 6:6-7 tells us we should live "in purity, understanding, patience **and kindness**; in the Holy Spirit and in sincere love; in truthful speech and in the power of God; with weapons of righteousness in the right hand and in the left."

And 2 Peter1: 5-7 says, "For this very reason, make every effort to add to your faith goodness; and to goodness, knowledge; and to knowledge, self-control; and to self-control, perseverance; and to perseverance, godliness, and to godliness, brotherly **kindness**; and to brotherly kindness, love.

Do you see somebody who is wrestling with anxiety? Don't just ignore them or say, "Don't be miserable." Draw alongside them and comfort them with kind words. When you do this, you are honouring the Lord. Your kind words might make all the difference.

Proverbs 12:25 says, "An anxious heart weighs a man down, but a **kind word** cheers him up."

But the real reason we should be kind, isn't to look for rewards or visible signs that our kindness has actually achieved anything. We may never know. The reason we want to be kind is because God wants us to be kind, and when we are kind, we honour Him.

As it says in Proverbs 14:13, "whoever is kind to the needy honours God."

So let us set our hearts on honouring the one who saved us from our sins, who never leaves us or forsakes us and meets our need. Let us make conscious effort to "Make sure that we never back wrong for wrong, but always try to be kind to each other and to everyone else." (1 Thessalonians 5:15)

6 Goodness

Ephesians 5:9 says, "For the fruit of the Spirit is in all **goodness** and righteousness and truth"

And 2 Chronicles 6:41 says, "be clothed with salvation, may your saints rejoice in your **goodness.**"

That is all very well, but what is goodness?

These days we use the word "good" so often it has almost lost its original meaning. For instance, we say, "Good morning." When we mean, "we hope you have a pleasant morning." We say, "good dog." When we mean, "You are an obedient dog." And we say someone is a "good husband" or "good wife", because they are faithful and look after their spouse." That is a lot of different meanings for one word, and I am sure you can think of others.

So that brings me back to my question, what is goodness?

and what has it got to do with the Holy Spirit?

Goodness in the Bible means, holiness, purity and righteous.
In short it means to have a Christ like nature. Does this take effort on our side? Of course, it does.

That is why 2 Peter 1:5
Tells us, "For this very reason, make every effort to add to your faith **goodness.**"

Can we be good on our own? Well, we can go through the motions. We can be kind, we can say the right things, we can avoid sinful things. But that doesn't necessary mean we are good and pure on the inside.

God wants our goodness to start on the inside and work its way out. That is why He gives us the Holy Spirit fruit of goodness in our spirits so that we are able to be pure and good from the inside out.

How can we help ourselves? By strengthening ourselves from the Bible.
2 Thessalonians 1:11 encourages us with these words, "Wherefore also we pray always for you, that our God would count you worthy of this calling, and fulfil all the good pleasure of his **goodness,** and the work of faith with power"

Will we always succeed in our quest to be good? No. But when we fail, we should go to God in prayer and ask Him to forgive us, and when we do this with a penitent heart, God lifts us up brushes down and encourage us to try again.

As it says in Psalm 34 :23-24, "the steps of a good man are ordered by the Lord, and He delights in his way. Though he falls he will not be cast down for the Lord uphold him with His Hand."

And did you know that when you let the goodness of God fill your heart, and act accordingly, people can see it on the outside? I remember shopping one Saturday morning when I saw a man and his wife, with their children, who were also shopping. I had never seen them before, but I saw something in their countenance that made me think, "I bet they are Christians." Next day at we had a guest speaker. You've guessed it, it was the same man I had seen in the shop!

Paul must have experienced the same thing when he said to the church in Rome, "I myself am convinced, my brothers, that you yourselves are full of goodness.' (Romans 15:14)

So, do we love and trust the Lord enough to want to take on this wonderful part of His character? Let us say "yes" to Him and then we can say with the Psalmist, "Surely, goodness and love will follow me all the days of my life," (Psalm 23:6)

7 Faithfulness

When we talk about faithfulness, we usually think of our own faithfulness to God. I remember when my mother used to hear the church bells ringing, she would say that they were, "calling the faithful to church." She may have been right, but to have any security in our faith, we must realise that God is always faithful to **us!**

We have to know that God is faithful in His promise to forgive when we give our hearts to Jesus. We have to know that that no matter how difficult life get that He will, "never leave us or forsake us." As it says in Hebrews 13:5.

To realise how faithful God is, we have to meditate on the wonderful things he has already done in our lives. When we do, we can say with the hymn writer, "through many dangers toils and snares, I have already come, 'tis grace that brought me safe thus far, and grace will lead me home."

The more we dwell on God's goodness the more we realise the truth of the Psalmists words, when he said, "But you, O Lord, are a compassionate and gracious God, slow to anger, abounding in love and **faithfulness**." (Psalm 86:15)

God is always faithful. Doesn't such faithfulness deserve our faithfulness in return? No matter what our Christian walk asks of us shouldn't we be faithful to our calling?

Joshua 24:14 says, "Now fear the Lord and serve him with all **faithfulness."**

So often we feel, "yes, I want to serve the Lord with all my being!" but how often do we lose our zeal and forget our promises to God?

Even here we can see the faithfulness of God, because He knows we can't do it on our own. That is why He endows us with the fruit of faithfulness, that by the power of His Holy Spirit we can have the strength to be as faithful to God as He is to us.

It isn't easy. There are so many other things tugging at us

we can easily slip out of our walk with God without even realising it. That is why Paul prayed the Church of Ephesus" "I pray that out of his glorious riches he may strengthen you with power through his Spirit in your inner being, so that Christ may dwell in your hearts through faith. " (Ephesians 3:16-17).

So, what do we do? How do we develop faithfulness? We start off in small ways, like making sure we read our Bibles regularly. We don't neglect fellowship. I know some people say you don't need to go to church to be a Christian, and that might be true, but you can't grow as a Christian without coming under the preaching of God's word.

Also, we need to spend time with God on our own. A quiet time Where He can minister to us and strengthen our resolve. Where we can confess our failures and asking Him to forgive us and strengthen us in our walk with Him.

And did you know that we have such a loving Heavenly Father, that not only does he help us to be faith, but He also rewards us when we are. 1 Samuel 26:23 says,"The LORD rewards every man for his righteousness and f**aithfulness**." How amazing is that?

So let us endure in our faithfulness to God and faithful to the words we say to each other, and faithful to the promises we make. Let us follow the example of our Lord and Saviour who was faithful even to death on the cross.

8 Gentleness

I think that if we want to be taken seriously as Christians, gentleness is a quality we all need to develop.

I remember hearing the testimony of an American who had

once been a gangster. He had lived a life of violence and knew no other way.

Eventually he was arrested and imprisoned for several years. While he was in prison, he became a Christian and he wanted to lead others to Christ, but he had no idea how to do it. So he did it the only way he knew how, with violence!

He was a big strong man, and he would approach a person he wanted to witness to and ask them if they wanted to become a Christian. If they said no, he would pick them up and keep slamming them against the wall until they said yes.

Fortunately for him and for all the inmates, one day the prison chaplain saw him doing it and drew him to one side to explain where he was going wrong.

Over time, the chaplain led this man prayerfully through the Bible, teaching hIm the necessary of gentleness, and as these teachings, because of his love for Jesus, he allowed the Holy to change him. So much so that this hardened violet man, became so gentle his complete countenance changed from one of hatred to one of gentleness. So much so that he to be re-photographed for his records because he had become unrecognisable from his original mug shot.

Surely, if God can make such a change in a man like that, he can do the same for us if we let Him.

Ephesians 4:2 says, "Be completely humble and **gentle;** be patient, bearing with one another in love."

We might say, "that's not the way I am, I like to tell it as it is."
Well we can tell it like it is in a gentle inoffensive way.

Or we might day, "I don't suffer fools gladly."
Isn't that just an excuse to be rude to somebody?
Philippians 4:5 tells us, "Let your **gentleness** be evident to all."
Doesn't that include fools as well? And let's face it, haven't we all been fools at some time in our lives? Especially before we invited Jesus into lives.

When I sin and I turn to Jesus for forgiveness, He doesn't treat me harshly, He gently corrects me and puts me back on the right path. Shouldn't we show this same grace to others? When someone is down we should be the first person to pick them up. Gently.

There is much anger in the world to, so much wrath. But did you know a gentle word turns wrath away. How will people be able to tell us apart from non-Christians if we act the same way as the world does?

Colossians 3:12 says, "Therefore, as God's chosen people, holy and dearly loved, clothe yourselves with compassion, kindness, humility, **gentleness** and patience."

The wonderful thing is, because we have the Holy Spirit within us, we have the ability to clothe ourselves in these things.

The world wants to be angry and judgemental, and condemning, that is why there is no peace to be found in the ways of the word, but 1Timothy 6:11says, "But you, man of God, flee from all this, and pursue righteousness, godliness, faith, love, endurance and **gentleness**".

We don't fight our battles in the way the world fights. We fight hatred with love, and anger with peaceful words, and pride with humility, and hostility with gentleness.

1 Peter says, 'But in your hearts, set apart Christ as Lord. Always be prepared to give an answer to everyone who asks you to give the reason for the hope that you have. But do this with **gentleness** and respect,"

We won't win anyone for Christ if we are not gentle with them, so let us nurture this fruit in our lives.

9 **Self control**

You will have notice that if we nurture all of the glorious fruit that God has planted in us through the divine power of His Holy Spirit, we are slowly but surely taking on the very nature of Christ, which should be the desire of all Christians. But we can ruin it all if we do not have self control.

That is why peter says, "For this very reason, make every effort to add to your faith goodness; and to goodness, knowledge; [6] and to knowledge, **self-control**." (2 Peter 1:5-6)

It is no use losing our temper with someone then saying, "it wasn't my fault, they made me los my temper."

Isn't that what wife beaters and murderers say? "They drove me to it."

How many of us sin because when we are tempted, instead of using our self-control, we allow ourselves to be led astray? All of us at some time in our lives I should imagine.

Proverbs 25:28 says, "Like a city whose walls are broken

down is a man who lacks self-control."

Think about it If we do not have self-control then we are not in control of our own lives. That is scary, isn't it? So what do we do about it? 1 Peter 5:8 says" Be **self-controlled** and alert. Your enemy the devil prowls around looking for someone to devour."

Who does the devil desire to devour? Christians of course. And He will do anything he can to ruin you testimony. If he temps us to sin and we have no self-control, we are easy meat.

To start off with we must take responsibility for our own actions. If we keep blaming others for making us sin we have learned nothing and never will.

It isn't good enough to pray, 'lord give me self-control.' He has already given it. It is up to us to use it.

Self control takes effort. That is why it is called self **control.** But the good news is The Holy Spirit aids us in our efforts.

In 1 Thessalonians 5:6 it says, "So then, let us not be like others, who are asleep, but let us be alert and self-controlled."

If the Lord tells us to do something it is because He knows that we can do it, even if we have never been self-controlled before it.

There are some things that we can do to help ourselves. For instance, if our friends will only lead us astray, we need to change our friends. If the places we go to causes us to sin, don't go to those places.

Titus 2:2 says, "Teach the older men to be temperate, worthy of respect, self-controlled, and sound in faith, in love and in endurance."

And Titus 2:6 says, "Similarly, encourage the young men to be self-controlled."

How can we teach anyone self -control if we haven't got it ourselves. We owe it to ourselves to be self-controlled, we owe it to our families to be self-controlled but most of all we owe it to our Lord and Saviour Jesus to be self-controlled.

So let us examine ourselves and be honest with ourselves. Is there part of our nature that is lacking in self-control? If there is let's confess it and work on it with the help of the Holy Spirit. Let us be more than conquerors in Jesus!

Let's talk about

Spiritual
Warfare

Some people shy away from the thought of spiritual warfare; it sounds frightening. They are frightened that the devil will do terrible things to them, and they won't be able to do a thing about it. I want to assure you, that just isn't true at all.

Jesus defeated Satan at Calvary when He died on the cross and they rose again on the third day.

When Jesus died, Satan thought he had won, but he was sadly mistake, Jesus broke Satan's power when He rose from the dead Hallelujah! And did you know that the same power that raised Christ from the dead (the Holy Spirit) is at work within you. (Ephesians 1:19).
Yes, the most powerful force on Earth is fighting your corner. God is on your side!

As it says in the following verses, **"If God is for us, who can be against us? ...... Who shall separate us from the love of Christ? Shall tribulation, or distress, or persecution, or famine, or nakedness, or peril, or sword? ....**
 Yet in all these things <u>we are more than conquerors through Him who loved us.</u> For I am persuaded that neither death nor life, nor angels nor principalities nor powers, nor things present nor things to come, nor height nor depth, nor any other created thing, shall be able to separate us from the love of God which is in Christ Jesus our Lord"   Romans 8: 31, 35, 37-39
The war is already won. Jesus won it for us. Now it is up to us, with the help of the Holy Spirit, to win the battles set before us.

Part 1
Know your Enemy

No one can go into battle if they don't know who their enemy is, so let's see what the Bible says about that.

Ephesians 6:12 says, "For we wrestle not against flesh and blood, but against principalities, against powers, against the rulers of the darkness of this world, against spiritual wickedness in high places."

"Not against flesh and blood"
This does not mean to say that Christians have no enemies among men that oppose them, even today many people suffer persecution and even death for their faith.

Nor does it mean that we don't have to contend with the carnal and corrupt desires of our old nature, which of course we do.

What it does mean is that our main battle is with the invisible spirits of wickedness that seek to destroy us. They are the source and origin of all our spiritual conflicts, and with them the warfare has to be maintained.

"But against principalities"
"There can be no doubt whatever that the apostle alludes here to evil spirits. Like good angels, they were regarded as divided into ranks and orders, and were supposed to be under the control of one mighty leader (Satan).
It is probable that the allusion here is to the ranks and orders which they sustained before their fall, something like which they may still retain. The word "principalities" refers to principal rulers, or chieftains."

"Powers"
Let us not forget that Satan is powerful, and we cannot defeat him on our own.

"Against the rulers of the darkness of this world"
This is a reference to pagan religions that have flourished throughout the world since time began, with human sacrifices and ancestor worship etc.

"Against spiritual wickedness"

" Literally, "The spiritual things of wickedness;" but the

allusion is undoubtedly to evil spirits, and to their influences on earth."

"In high places"

The Bible teaches us that evil spirits occupy the lofty regions of the air, for instance the Prince of Persia mentioned in Daniel 10:13.
It is believed by many Christians that these forces of evil rule over countries and with all their malignant influences, keeping the people in fear and darkness. It is against these powers that Christians are called to contend.

But take heart, we are not in this battle alone, God knows that we couldn't cope on our own,
That is why in 2 Chronicles 20:15 it says, "Do not be afraid or discouraged ... for the battle is not yours but the Lord's."

Part Two
<u>Know the Enemies Characteristics</u>

Let's look at what the Bible says about the devil
He is a liar.
John 8:44 says, "for he (the devil) is a liar and the father of it."

So many people have fallen for the lies of Satan. We don't have to because we have the Spirit of truth (the Holy Spirit in us. Also, we have the Bible to teach us the truth of God's word.

He is a thief.
John 10:10 "The thief does not come except to steal, and to kill, and to destroy. I have come that they may have life."

The devil will steal all we have if we let him, especially our joy and peace of mind, but we have the fruit of the Spirit in us. We can keep our peace and joy if we just remember to trust the Lord in all things and keep our faith in Him.

He is the accuser of the Christians.
Did you know that the devil has the audacity to go before God and accuse us of sins? We see a good example of that in the story of Job. But don't worry about that, God already know about our sins and He has forgiven them. there is good news about that in
Rev 12:10 says, "For the accuser of our brothers and sisters (in Jesus) who accuses them before God, day and night, has been cast down."
Praise the Lord, God has already dealt with that one. And if God won't listen to him neither must we when he tries to tell us we are not worthy of God's love because we our sinners. God has already forgiven our sins, have been made

whole in Christ.

He is master of disguise.
2 Cor 11:14 says, "For Satan himself transforms himself into an angel of light."
 Let us beware, if we start to wander from our faith and start looking elsewhere for answer, the devil will give us answers, He will appear like a guiding light to us to lead us astray. Just like he did to Eve in the Garden of Eden.
This is so many strange cults get started. Satan convinces people that if they follow his teachings all will go well for them. A word of wisdom for all of us; no matter how good something looks, if it disagrees with the Bible, it is wrong. Don't touch it.

He is like a roaring lion.
1 Peter 5:8 tells us, "Your adversary the devil walks about like a roaring lion, seeking whom he may devour."

that sounds scary doesn't it? But don't worry, how to handle that one is found in
James 4:7 encourages us with these words,
"Submit yourselves, then to God. Resist the devil and He will flee from you."

He can roar all he likes, but if we submit to God the devil doesn't get a look in!

He is a tempter.
 In Matthew 4:1 read this,
"Then Jesus was led up by the Spirit into the wilderness to be tempted by the devil."

The devil will always try to ruin our walk with God by tempting us to sin. Don't fall for it. So often people fall for his tempting lies and think, "It's ok, no one will ever find

out."
Only for the devil bring their sins out into the open and bring sorrow and disgrace into their lives. Let us not fall for his seductive lies, let us learn how to use the self-control we have been blessed with.

Sometimes temptation seems so hard to resist, doesn't it? That is why Matt 26:41 tells us
"Watch and pray, lest you enter into temptation"

Having said that, should you fall for temptation, as soon as you realise what you have done, turn to God and confess it. Don't allow the devil to make you think you have lost your salvation, God is always ready to forgive us, pick us up and brush us down, and help us to start a fresh walk with Him. Remember, you are a child of God. What loving father ever turns his children away when they come back to him in repentance for their failures?

The long and the short of it is, Satan's aim is, to destroy the church and to bring death suffering and misery where every he can. If he cannot destroy us, he does his best to render us in effective. He will use all his whiles to bring this about.

We must beware of his tactics. Here are some of them.

The seat of Satan's attack is always our mind.

He will play on our weaknesses.

He will bring division where he can.

He will use our ignorance against us and play on our fears.

He tries to make us feel unworthy, or to do the opposite and make us feel proud and therefore become arrogant.

He tells us we have a right to hold grudges and unforgiveness in our hearts.

He tries to bring legalism into the Church.

He sows seeds of apathy.

He will do anything to rob us or make us unaware of <u>**our strength and power through Jesus Christ!**</u>

Don't believe a word of his lies. I believe Jesus, and Jesus said. **"I will build my Church and all the powers of Hell will not conquer it."** (Matthew 16:18 New living translation)

Brothers and sisters, realise this, we are on the winning side, Jesus has already won the war against Satan.

Part Three
Know Your Protection

God wants us to know that we are protected against are enemy, and because our battle is a spiritual battle, God provides us with spiritual armour.

So that people could understand this armour Paul compared it to the armour that people would see every day on the Roman Soldier.

Of course, physical armour in useless in spiritual warfare, so let's look at how God replaces it with spiritual armour.

We read about it in Ephesians 6:11.

Helmet of
Salvation

Breastplate of
Righteousness

Belt of Truth

Shield of Faith

Sword of
the Spirit

Shoes of the
Gospel of Peace

The armour of God

Ephesians 6:10-11
"Put on the whole armour of God, that you may be able to

stand against the wiles of the devil."

Ephesians 6:14-17
"Stand firm then with a belt of truth buckled round your waist; with the breastplate of righteousness in place and with your feet fitted with the readiness of that comes from a gospel of peace. In addition to all this take up the shield of faith with which you can extinguish all the flaming arrows of the evil one. Take the helmet of Salvation and the sword of the spirit which is the word of God."

Let's look at these things individually.

The belt of truth.

The belt, or girdle as it is sometimes known. it kept all the other pieces in place. And it is the same with the belt of truth that keeps our Heavenly armour in place.
Jesus said, "You will know the truth and the truth shall set you free." (John 8 :32)
So what is the truth?
John 14:6 Jesus says "I am the way, The Truth and the life"
That's right, we are putting on Jesus as we go into battle.!
As we have already said, Jesus has already beaten the enemy; we have nothing to fear.
It is His truth we need. In our battle we need to live in the truth of God's Word, at the same time being truthful and honest ourselves. If we are not truthful with God, truthful with others and truthful with ourselves, we are leaving a chink in our armour where the enemy can attack.

The breastplate of righteousness

Christ is our righteousness.
It was because He was pure and sinless that He was the

only one who could die in our place at Calvary.
But also, we must strive to live righteous lives, or once again we are leaving a chink in our armour. Remember if you do sin, repent of it quickly before you allow Satan to use it against you.

With your feet fitted with the readiness of that comes from a gospel of peace.

It seems funny to talk about peace when we are talking spiritual warfare doesn't it?
But we are not talking about peace with the devil, far from it. Satan wants to steal our peace of mind so cannot concentrate on our battle with.
We need to have good strong footwear that will not let us slip in battle. Our battle is against the lies of Satan, so we must have a firm footing in the Gospel of Christ.

Our enemy hates people having peace. Let us have a readiness to share the wonderful peace of the Gospel of Christ, the gospel that brings peace with God, with everyone we can.

Above all taking the shield of faith

"Above all" does not mean "most important of all," but "to cover all." A soldier holds his
shield to defend himself. It constitutes a protection over every part of his body, as it can be turned in every direction. The idea is, that as the shield covered or protected the other parts of the armour, so faith had a similar importance in the Christian virtues.
The shield was an ingenious device by which blows, and arrows might be parried off, and the whole body defended. It could be made to protect the head, or the heart, or thrown behind to meet all attack there. As long as the

soldier had his shield, he felt secure; and as long as a Christian has faith, he is secure.
Secure in the knowledge that Jesus will never leave us or forsake us. Secure that the battle belongs to the Lord and He will fight it for us.

The helmet of salvation

The helmet defended the head, a vital part, and so the helmet of salvation will defend our minds and keep it from the blows of the enemy.

WE ARE SAVED!

Keep that thought in your head. The devil will try to rob of that thought with his lies. Don't listen to him. Keep God's promises in your mind and heart.

IF GOD SAYS YOU ARE SAVED THEN YOU ARE SAVED. End of story, and the devil can do nothing about it

Part four
Know your Weapons!

 Ok, so we know who our enemy is and his tactics, and we know about our armour, but to win battles we need weapons.

In 2 Cor 10:4-5 it says,
 "For the weapons of our warfare are not carnal but mighty in God for pulling down strongholds, casting down arguments and every high thing that exalts itself against the knowledge of God, bringing every thought into captivity to the obedience of Christ.

So, what are these weapons? Let's look at them.

Prayer
Never doubt the importance of prayer.
James 5:16-18 says,
 "The effective, fervent prayer of a righteous man avails much. Elijah was a man with a nature like ours, and he prayed earnestly that it would not rain; and it did not rain on the land for three years and six months."

When you read that you might think, "yeah, but he was a righteous man. I'm not. I have to disagree with you there. Do you believe God? Of course, you do that is why you are reading this.
Romans 4 :3 says, "Abraham believed God and it was counted to him as righteousness."

Never think that your prayers don't make a difference. They do. **Your** prayers change things.

Jesus reminds us of that in **Mark 11:24**

"Therefore, I say to you, whatever things you ask when you pray, believe that you receive them, and you will have them."

That is interesting, isn't it? We don't just have to pray, we must actually **believe** that that God is going to answer them. So, we have a choice, don't we? We can either believe God will answer our prayers or we can believe He isn't going to answer them. It is just as easy to believe one as the other, so let us choose to believe God will answer our prayers.

.

The word of God

Yes, the word of God, the Bible, is not only part of our spiritual enemy, but also a weapon to be used against the devil.

We read in Matt 4:1-4 "Then Jesus was led up by the Spirit into the wilderness to be tempted by the devil. And when He had fasted forty days and forty nights, afterward He was hungry. Now when the tempter came to Him, he said, "If You are the Son of God, command that these stones become bread." But He answered and said, "It is written ...."
Three times the devil tried to temp Jesus, and three times Jesus just quoted scripture to him, until in the end the devil departed from him.

The devil cannot argue against the word, but a word of warning, the devil knows what the Bible says, and he will try to confuse you by mis-quoting the Bible to you. Try hard to get to know your Bible, and if something it says causes you to worry, speak to an older Christian and ask the to make it clear to you

The name of Jesus
Did you know that there is actual power in using the name of Jesus? Look at what happened when the lame man, who had been lame since birth, asked Peter and John for money.

Acts 3:4-7 "Peter looked straight at him did John. The Peter said, "Look at us" so the man gave them his attention expecting to receive something from them. Then Peter said, "Silver and gold I do not have, but what I do have I give you: In the name of Jesus Christ of Nazareth, rise up and walk." Taking him by the right hand he helped him up, and instantly the man's feet and ankles became strong."

Wow that's powerful stuff, isn't it? Peter didn't heal that man in his own strength, he never had the power. It was the name of Jesus that brought healing to that man.

Acts 16:18 tells us the story of a girl possessed of an evil spirit was delivered by Paul. It reads, "But Paul, greatly annoyed, turned and said to the spirit, "I command you in the name of Jesus Christ to come out of her."
And he came out that very hour. Do you know why?

Phil 2:10-11 explains it.
 "At the name of Jesus every knee should bow, of those in Heaven, and of those on earth, and of those under the earth."

That is right, the name of Jesus is so powerful that

everything must yield to it. Demons' quiver at the name of Jesus because they have no power against it.

The anointing of the Holy Spirit
1 John 4:4-5
He who is in you is greater than he who is in the world.
We already know this don't we from what we read before.

Our obedience

I bet you have never considered obedience as a weapon before, have you? But it is one, our obedience very often activates God's power. Do you need more convincing? Well look at the story of Gideon, it is in Judges Chapter 6-8.

You can read it for yourself, but the gist of is that the Israelites were under the rule of the Midianites who were a cruel and vindictive people.

One day Gideon was threshing wheat in a winepress; He had to do it in a secret place where the Midianites couldn't steal it from him. While he was working an angel appeared to him and said, "The Lord is with you mighty warrior. The Lord is going to use you to save Israel out of the Midian's Hand."

Gideon thought that was ridicules and said so
He said, "My clan is the weakest in Manasseh, and I am the weakest in my family, how can I save Israel?"

That was a good question, wasn't it? What could he do? Well, he did the only thing he could do that could bring victory, he obeyed what God told him to do. As a result, he defeated the Midianite army of countless thousands with only three hundred men! It is an amazing story read it for yourself if you haven't already done so.

But the point I am making is this, it wasn't Gideon's strength that won the battle, it was his obedience.

There are many stories in the Bible that follow the same theme, it was only by being obedient that brought about victory. Because he was obedient, Abraham became the father of a nation. Because he was obedient, Moses led the children of Israel out of slavery. Because Jonah was obedient (eventually) he brought a whole city to repentance and saved them from destruction.

But the greatest act of obedience ever was when Jesus went to the cross to be crucified. The night before in the garden of Gethsemane, Jesus had prayed, "Father take this cup fresh me." Meaning the need to die on the cross. But then he added the words that would change everything, "Nevertheless your will not mine."

That amazing act of obedience changed the whole of the world for everyone. In doing it Jesus defeated death and opened up Heaven for everyone who would put their trust in Him. Oh, hallelujah and a thousand more hallelujahs.

So, what is God telling to do today that seems far beyond our capabilities. Firstly, check out that it really is from God. That is what. Gideon did. One night he laid a fleece on the ground and said to the Lord, if this is really of you Lord when the morning comes let the ground around the fleece be wet with dew but the fleece be dry." So God did.
Just to be sure, on the following night Gideon said, " if it really is of you this time let the fleece be soaked with dew but the ground around it be dry."
When God did that as well, Gideon knew it was from the Lord and did what he was told to do.
So let's not be afraid to ask God to verify what He is telling us to do, and when He does whatever it is, let us be obedient and do it with all our strength, so that we may

have the victory.

Praising God

However could praising be a weapon against the devil you may well ask?

 David knew the power of praise. In Psalm 103:1-2 he says, "Praise the Lord oh my soul, and everything within me praise His Holy name. Praise the Lord oh my soul and forget not all His benefits."

When we are going through difficult times it can be difficult to praise the Lord can't it? Our eyes are on the problem, not on the Lord. And that is how the devil likes it!

He loves to keep our minds on the bad things, that way he can rob us of hope, rob us of our joy and leave us feeling depressed. Oh how happy that makes him.

When we start to praise the Lord and tank Him for all the wonderful things that He has already done, things start to happen.

For a start gratitude starts to arise in our hearts. We realise how mighty and wonderful our Lord. Our hearts start to lift, and the depression starts to fade and be replaced by faith. God has never let me down before; He is not going to start now.

WE no longer have our eyes on the problem but on the one who can deliver us from our problems. God is glorified and the devil loses his grip on our emotions. No wonder that when the Israelites were going into battle against the Benjamites in Judges chapter 20 God told them to send Judah first. Judah means praise. God wanted them to go into battle praising Him so that they could be confident of victory because they knew He would be their strength.

I am absolutely certain that praising God is a wonderful weapon against the enemy.

Prayer

Oh, the mountains that have been moved and the strongholds that have been broken down by prayer.

James chapter 5; 16 tells us, "The prayer of a righteous person is powerful and effective.'
As I have said before we have been made righteous through Jesus, therefore that means us.
Then just to get this point across, in verse 17 James continues. "Elijah was a human being even as we are. He prayed earnestly that it would not rain, and it did not rain on the land for three and a half years. Again, he prayed, and the heavens gave rain, and the earth produced crops."

Don't you think that is amazing? I do. How could one man's prayers have such an effect?

Phil 4:5-7 tells us,
"Be anxious for nothing, but in everything by prayer and supplication, with thanksgiving, let your requests be made known to God; and the peace of God, which surpasses all understanding, will guard your hearts and minds through Christ Jesus. "

Part five

Strategies for Victorious Living

Be Vigilant
1 Peter 5:8-9 says,
"Be sober, be vigilant; because your adversary the devil walks about like a roaring lion, seeking whom he may devour."

Put on the armour of God daily
Eph 6:11-1"Put on the whole armour of God, that you may be able to stand against the wiles of the devil."

Submit to God
James 4:7-8 "Therefore, submit to God. Resist the devil and he will flee from you. Draw near to God and He will draw near to you."

Attend Church regularly.
Hebrews 10:24-25, And let us consider one another in order to stir up love and good works, not forsaking the assembling of ourselves together,
Strife to keep the unity of the Church

Love one another
John 13:34-35, new commandment I give to you, that you love one another; as I have loved you, that you also love one another. By this all will know that you are my disciples.

And finally, know who you are.

Rom 8:37-38 tells that, "In all these things **we are more than conquerors** through Him who loved us."

That means you, that means me, that means the whole church of God. When we are filled with the Holy Spirit, we can win every battle against the enemy.

So let's go forward into battle and bring
Glory to Jesus!

notes

About this book

The Holy Spirit is God on earth today!
When Jesus died on the cross the Calvary, it was for us. He died to save us from our sin and if we believe on him as our Lord and saviour, he has promised us a place in heaven when we die.

But what about the rest of our life on earth? How are we supposed to cope? God knows we can't live victoriously on our own, that is why Jesus sent the Holy Spirit, that we might be filled with him and be more than conquerors.

But who is the Holy Spirit?

What are his gifts and his fruit?

What is spiritual warfare and how are we going to win every battle?

Let's talk about all these things in this book.